8/21/20

To Annette & Patrick,
Enjoy — Maureen

SOMEWHERE IN ITALY
V-MAILS FROM MY FATHER

Dad with orphaned children

First Sergeant Robert E. Bell, United States Army WWII

September 1943 - June 1945

Maureen Bell Broglia

Dad's dream was to return to Italy one day

It made me sad that he was never able to take that trip

But now he can go wherever he wants said my young daughter

The story of Robert E. Bell is a gift to my family

So they know

©2018

This book may not be reproduced, either in part or in its entirety, in any form, by any means, without written permission from the publisher or author, with the exception of brief excerpts for purposes of radio, television, or published review. All rights, including the right of translation are reserved.

ISBN# 978-1-945853-08-1
Marriah Publishing
122 Manners Road
Ringoes, NJ 08551

TABLE OF CONTENTS

Cover: Sgt. Bell in forefront sailing from North Africa into Naples Harbor October 23, 1943

Dedication Page 2

Introduction 6

Chapter I: Boot Camp 16

Chapter II: Road to Rome - Salerno, Naples, Volturno, Cassino, Anzio, Rome ... 23

Chapter III: 19 Days - from the Apennines to the Alps 39

Chapter IV: Walking in His Boots, Trip to Italy 2014 47

Chapter V: The Bell Family 50

Chapter VI: Aloha Dad 57

Introduction

SOLDIERS WRITING HOME - HANK AND DAD IN DOORWAY

How many times did I open that box?

It had traveled all over the country, beginning in Providence where the US Army sent Dad's belongings home in 1946 after the war. For over 70 years it made its way across the USA to rest in other homes . . . Franklin PA, Detroit MI, Jensen Beach Fl, Charlestown Beach RI, and eventually to Dad's final home and resting place, Ewa Beach Hawaii.

Where to begin? Why was I procrastinating?

In July of 2014, in desperation, I called my brother Michael. "Let's fly to Italy and find Dad's war."

A few months later I boarded a plane at JFK/NY heading for Rome. Mike and Lisa had arrived two days earlier from their home in Bali. We celebrated our reunion with wine from the local vineyards, slabs of prosciutto, Reggio Parmisano cheese and fresh mozzarella on bread still hot from the oven. Oh my God! No wonder Dad loved Italy. Another bottle of wine was uncorked . . . And then another . . .   The next day we began our 3-week pilgrimage from Rome to Anzio to Salerno to the Amalfi Coast and back up the boot to Firenze, Bologna, Milano and into the mountains and villages where our father fought. Our final destination was the magnificent Lake Garda. Astounding beauty!

Nearly two years had gone by following our excursion through Italy and I still couldn't write the story . . . Why was I still stuck? Was it possible that I just couldn't do it?

Then one morning I opened the closet, pulled out the box, and noticed for the first time a brown envelope with my Grandmother's writing:

"K.L. Hanson - Robbie Bell's V-Mails 1943-44."

As I read his V-Mails, I was riveted - feeling the heartbeat of the young brave soldier, laying on his cot under a tent, writing to his beloved family across the sea far away. More likely, he was lying in a muddy foxhole, wet and trembling in the cold dark terrifying mountains listening for the explosion of the next enemy attack.

The war in Italy was hell on earth. No kidding. Writing and reading his V-Mails from home had to be his sanity. The pulse of that young soldier became my pulse. And so the story finally began . . .

WHAT WERE V-MAILS?   Mail from our Soldiers to Family and Loved Ones at Home

What is black and white and red all over? Answer: V-Mail stationery

During World War II cargo space and weight on ships and planes was at a premium. Hundreds of heavy sacks of mail from our GI's to their families and loved ones back home took up too much valuable space on cargo containers. Mail was often held up in favor of supplies. To overcome the demoralizing effect on our men at war of not getting their mail delivered, the post office developed a process which shrunk standard- size paper and envelopes, utilizing microfilm processing, which produced Victory Mail, known as "V-Mail."

The processed copy replaced the original letter, saving valuable space and expediting the delivery of letters home to eagerly awaiting families. The microfilmed letters were printed on the receiving end in the USA. and then delivered to the families of our soldiers. A typical V-Mail was a single sheet of paper, measuring approximately 4-1/4 by 5 inches.

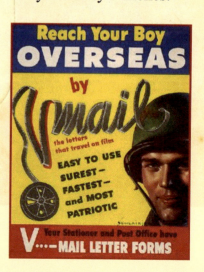

V-Mails from my Father, Sgt. Robert E. Bell

Christmas 1943 (left)
&
Christmas 1944 (right)

These are his original drawings.

"The Post Office, War, and Navy Departments realize fully that frequent and rapid communication with parents, associates, and other loved ones strengthens fortitude, enlivens patriotism, makes loneliness endurable, and inspires to even greater devotion, the men and women who are carrying on our fight far from home. We know that the good effect of expeditious mail service on those of us at home is immeasurable."
- from the Annual Report of the U.S. Postmaster General, 1942

Mail to our American Armed Forces Overseas

Victory Mail, more commonly known as V-Mail, operated during World War II to expedite mail service for **American armed forces overseas.** Moving the rapidly expanding volume of wartime mail posed hefty problems for the Post Office and War Departments. Officials sought to reduce the bulk and weight of letters, and found a model in the British Airgraph Service, started in 1941, that microfilmed messages for dispatch. V-Mail used standardized stationery and microfilm processing to produce lighter, smaller cargo. Space was made available for other war supplies and more letters could reach military personnel faster around the globe. This new mode of messaging was launched on June 15, 1942. V-Mail assisted with logistical issues while acknowledging the value of communication. In 41 months of operation, letter writers using the system provided a significant lifeline between the frontline and home.

A Brief History

The first letter sheets were printed with black ink when the V-Mail service began operations on June 15, 1942. A more vibrant red soon replaced the somber black. As well as being more patriotic in look, the red also helped to flag the V-Mail letters for sorting, processing, and preferential transport.

The stationery was custom designed to meet the functions of V-Mail service, which postal and military officials introduced to handle the dramatic increase in wartime overseas mail exchanges. V-Mail used standardized stationery and microfilm processing to produce lighter, smaller cargo. Less space needed for mail made more space available for other war supplies. And, more letters could reach their destination faster around the globe. The lighter letters (whether dispatched in original form or microfilmed) allowed V-Mail to travel aboard swift airplanes rather than slow boats.

As an aerogramme made for air transport, V-Mail forms combined the letter and envelope into one single sheet. The earliest forms, in addition to being printed in black, filled one entire side with instructions for use while the opposite side provided space for addresses, censor marks, and correspondence. That was fine for microfilming, but not for mailing. To convert the form into a more effective envelope, officials reduced the instruction text and added space for addresses and postage.

In addition, working as an efficient, light-weight mailing piece, the letter sheet also had to meet the specifications for the microfilm equipment. The 8½ by 11 inch sheet had to be of uniform weight, grade, and grain to fit in the Eastman Kodak Recordak machines used to copy letters to microfilm. For the majority of the service's operations, 20-pound paper was used. A 16-pound paper was developed later with the opacity and the durability required for microfilming. The number of sheets per pound increased from 90 to 120. Officials estimated that microfilm saved up to 98% on cargo space.

To encourage the use of V-Mail, the Post Office Department and the military made the stationery available for free to the armed forces and civilians. Patrons could get two sheets per day from their local post office. The Government Printing Office (GPO) supplied the stationery. In addition, private companies with postal permits printed the letter sheets. The permit number or GPO mark was generally placed in the bottom right margin.

The Sheaffer Company produced a clever packaging format, selling a mailable tube filled with V-Mail stationery, ink, and other writing necessaries. The paper's design allowed for maximum space for the correspondent's writings. Between 300 handwritten and 700 typed words could fit between margins required for the microfilm processing and below the lines for addresses and the spot for the censor's stamp.

But not all writers had to face filling in a blank page. Pre-printed contents also came readily available in a variety of cartoons, holiday messages, official change of address forms, and more. **Units with talented artists (see Dad's artwork on page 9!) and access to printing facilities produced V-Mail sheets with greetings. The Seabees, Naval Construction Battalions, often replaced the usual "V-Mail" in the bottom margin with their own name.**

Use of V-Mail began to decline in the spring of 1945 and microfilming ceased November 1, 1945.

Who was Ma Hanson?

Katherine Louise Hanson was my maternal grandmother. How very fortunate for the Bell family that she saved all of her V-mails from my Dad during WWII. They have deeply enriched the memory and war history of First Sgt. Robert E. Bell - indeed a treasure. All other V-mails back and forth to Italy were either lost or destroyed.

As the eldest grandchild, I knew her well. She loved movies and the theater and shopping in Providence and train trips to Boston to special events. Always "on the go" - I loved that about her! Our routine was lunch at a Chinese restaurant and dessert at the end of our day at Shepard's Tea Room.

I stayed with her often overnight at her house in Riverside; especially during the war. I remember vividly her small library of beautiful old books. What happened to them? On a nice day we would drop in on her neighborhood friends who would overload me with candy, cookies and soda. I was a living poster child. My dad was fighting overseas for our country.

Her background was Alsatian/Irish. Her father, Theodore Mueller, was from Strasbourg, Germany. Her mother was Mary Ellen Creegan. Nana was schooled in both French and German and as a young girl wrote and translated letters to and from Europe - mostly to Fr. Andre, a benedictine monk who was her father's brother.

And last but not least, she had a hat fetish. Each time she added a new one for her collection she would take a snapshot of herself in a photo booth at the Providence train station. The photos below are just a few of them. My Aunt Natalie said that she actually had her hats insured!

1918   1930's   1944   1956

About Stars and Stripes ... During World War II, this news source was printed in dozens of editions in several operating theaters. Both newspapermen in uniform and young soldiers, some of whom would later become important journalists, filled the staffs and showed zeal and talent in publishing and delivering the publications on time. Some of the editions were assembled and printed very close to the battlegrounds to get the latest, most timely information to the troops. The newspaper also published a 53-book series of G.I. Stories.

Cartoonist Bill Mauldin did his his popular "Up Front" cartoons for the WWII publications of Stars and Stripes. Mauldin's characters, Willie & Jo and Sad Sack, were usually infantrymen, sometimes combat medics, and sometimes artillerymen. Always, they were haggard, unshaven, and full of the line soldiers' bitter pragmatism. A general officer once remarked, "Bill Mauldin is the greatest single morale factor in Italy and France next to food and clothing." Another high command general said that he considered Mauldin and Ernie Pyle the two greatest reporters of the war. Mauldin was the first authentic voice in WWII cartooning to gain recognition. When he returned home as an editorial cartoonist, he was honored as a two-time winner of the Pulitzer Prize. Mauldin'g mission was to forget the danger and misery of combat life. It was a fitting tribute to his honesty and greatness that he fulfilled that mission.

Bill Mauldin Cartoons

The Prince and the Pauper

"Wish to hell I wuzn't housebroke."

"Didn't we meet at Cassino?"

"I wuz beginnin' to think nobody wuz home."

"Hey Fritz, how far are the Russians from Berlin?"

"Hope it ain't a rocky beach. Me feet's tender since they got webbed."

"I'm lookin' fer turtle eggs, Junior."

"Must belong to a politician."

15th Field Artillery Battalion Observers Spot, Plot Nazi Guns
A Report by Stars and Stripes

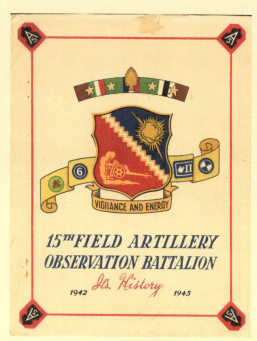

**The 15th FAOB
My Father's Battalion**

With the 5th Army, March 11, 1945 - After 16 consecutive months of combat duty in Italy, the highly trained flash, sound, and meteorological technicians of the 15th Field Observation Battalion spread out over the whole of the forward sector of II Corps on the highest peaks of the Apennines. They are still making trouble for enemy gun positions on the Italian front. It is the only American unit of its kind now fighting with the 5th Army.

On October 24, 1943, when men of the 15th Battalion occupied positions north of Naples near Pietravalrano, the unit started on this vital and specialized assignment. Sound and flash bases were established and survey parties were sent out. Observation posts were established on high vantage points. The meteorological section soon sent its first balloons aloft, and the skilled technicians began their relentless and fruitful search for the enemy guns with special equipment and more precise calculations than are used in the usual method of artillery observation.

During the bitter mountain fighting of the first Italian winter, the 15th moved its OPs methodically ahead from peak to peak as the fighting progressed northward. The greater part of its casualties however were suffered at the beachhead around Anzio. Some of its elements landed on the beach on D-day and others followed two days later.

By early February, the entire organization was entrenched at Anzio-Nettuno and, in spite of the incessant enemy shelling and bombing to which it was subjected, it unflinchingly continued operations, accounting for the location of 1,968 enemy gun positions and 93 other targets, including enemy tanks and infantrymen. It also furnished much metro, survey, and topographical data to the artillery and air corps.

When the beachhead forces drove across the flatlands for the final drive on Rome, the 15th took full part in the offensive. Fifty-three of its officers and men were awarded the Purple Heart, five wear the Legion of Merit and 21 were awarded Bronze Stars.

The 15th continued in its specialized mission through Rome, Montalto De Castro, Orbetello, and Grosseto. Northeast of Piombino, it swung north through Suvereto, Pomerance, Bagni Di Casciana and from there to Fiesole in the northeastern suburbs of Florence. Later, the battalion continued in the pursuit across the Arno, through the Gothic Line and into the Apennine Mountains, where, perched again upon high peaks and ridges, it is serving the Second Corps Artillery.

It is calculated that the 15th has spotted and plotted the positions of 4,096 enemy guns during its sixteen months of fighting in Italy, bringing about their destruction by effective counter battery fire or forcing their withdrawal from well prepared locations.

Chapter 1: Boot Camp

SGT BELL - CENTER - IN TRAINING AT MADISON BARRACKS

About Cartoonist Ernie Pyle

In 1942 after the United States entered World War II, Ernie Pyle served overseas as a war correspondent. He covered the North African campaign and the invasions of Sicily and Italy. He was awarded the Pulitzer Prize for distinguished correspondence, and in 1945 traveled to the Pacific to cover the war against Japan where he was killed by enemy fire on the island of Ie Shima. President Truman spoke of how Pyle "told the story of the American fighting men as they wanted it told."

Ernie Pyle is buried at the National Memorial Cemetery of the Pacific on the Hawaiian Island of Oahu. This is where his comrade, First Sgt. Robert E. Bell, is also buried - resting in peace together and forever.

Dad in training with 15th FOB (Field Observation Battalion) at Madison Barracks, Sackets Harbor, New York

In the Beginning: Fort Bragg, NC July 1942

Our battalion was not born of an impulsive fancy. Since 1923 the 15th Field Artillery Observation Battalion was a gleam in the eyes of the War Department. Our birth certificate is dated July 1, 1942 - the date of activation. Our first battalion commander was Lt. Col. Robert Hallick.

Activation occurred at Fort Bragg, North Carolina. At the end of July, 125 men crawled into a train leaving for Madison Barracks, New York. Accompanying the men were 21 officers. After two agonizing days the lid was rolled back and the men stumbled out of the train onto the soil of Sackets Harbor, NY.

Madison Barracks: Aug, 1942 - Feb 1943

Madison Barracks would be a soldier's paradise even without the help of the Hotel Woodruff in Watertown and the OG Grill in Sackets Harbor. The barracks overlooked Lake Ontario's Black River Bay. In the winter the Barracks and the surrounding country made up a large snow-bound outpost. Snow drifts reached for the sky and thermometers dropped to terrifying lows. Initial training was conducted in much the same vein as it had been at Fort Bragg and eventually resolved itself into well organized classes, drill periods and field exercises. Separate units specialized in communications and sound and flash ranging. Training was such that the battalion could put small groups familiar with most aspects of sound and flash ranging into the field at an early date.

The bitter cold and heavy snowfall of the winter months of '42 were not conducive to outdoor training. Nevertheless, familiarization courses with small arms had to be completed. Snow-blinded men spent hours frozen to the stocks of rifles and aiming into space on the Stony Point range. There were those who would not permit an icy drill field to go to waste. So, we chipped crooked lines on the ice and zigzagged and hopped around whenever such activity was in violation of civilian standards. These corps stamina tests also included a four-mile gallop over icy roads during our daily "casual hour" (Dad must have been dreaming about Hawaii back then).

During the cold weather, classroom work dominated the schedule. Sound rangers will remember the days spent on the theory and repair of a "cutter" which had gone sour.

In late February of 1943 it was announced that our days at the barracks were numbered. Training abruptly ceased in favor of packing and crating . . . A few million crates were stuffed with hydrogen generators, sound sets, flash spotting scopes, transits, and typewriters. We had finished our garrison life and were ready for the rugged outdoors.

AP Hill: March 1943 - June 1943

On March 16 1943 we set out for AP Hill Military Reservation, Virginia. The train bounced into Virginia on the 19th of March. It was a tired group that lay down to sleep under the star-studded Virginia sky. Tents would have been absurd. We wanted all the warm outdoors we could get after being cooped up in combat suits and boiler rooms at Madison Barracks. Before morning a disgruntled, snarling group of men was blanketed in snow ... Back to Virginia - at that time an observation battalion was still considered some peculiar bastard son of the artillery ... some type of organization that should have balloons but didn't.

Camp Forrest, Tennessee, June - July 1943 ... Chiggers!

On June 17 we left for Camp Forrest Tennessee for Second Army Maneuvers. We had thus far experienced only the pleasant side of outdoor life - now our education was to be rounded out. We arrived at 2 am and were fed ice cream and cookies. Otherwise the trip to Tennessee was uneventful ...

... When the rains subsided sufficiently for the chiggers to breathe without bubbling they got to work on us, paying particular attention to Sgt. Robinson who for weeks was an unrecognizable red mess of pimpled protoplasm. Men ate and sweated sulfur and they powdered themselves with sulfur until coins in their pockets turned black.

Although the fighting spirit of the battalion was definitely on the increase, it was decided to capitulate to the chiggers. We received orders to move on to Fort Dix, New Jersey.

Wild rumors were still with us and the only thing that was certain was that the battalion would NOT be sent overseas.

Fort Dix, New Jersey - July 17, 1943 "Out of the frying pan . . . ."

The battalion's stay at Fort Dix was possibly the most trying for the personnel, as many of them found the train travel quite tiring, especially when coming back to Dix for laundry, etc. before heading out again for New York, Philadelphia, and other civilian encampments. By the end of July, the battalion found itself far ahead of the road to accomplishing the mass of requirements necessary in staging operations. Under an umbrella of excitement men received immunization shots and fired carbine and pistol qualification courses, underwent physical conditioning, and packed and crated. Then we jogged past a few disinterested doctors for our final medical inspection. During the evening hours of Aug 19, in an atmosphere of extreme secrecy, the battalion was called out with each man in full field pack plus the Empire State building on his back . We then started toward Staten Island's Pier 16. Everyone blinked, gulped, muttered a short prayer, and then drew to an inside straight. On August 20 at 4 am with a cup of coffee and two Red Cross doughnuts in each man's upset stomach, and with no pretty girls throwing no pretty flowers as no band played, the battalion filed aboard the S.S. Parker in gangplank order. After that, there was no room for order of anything else.

Africa - August 20, 1943

Until the 3,000 troops had been squeezed aboard, it was thought that the capacity of the Jimmy Parker was 1,500. It took a little under two minutes from the time we got on the gangplank for all to be homesick. After depositing their gear below all the nervous men went on deck to take their last look at the New York skyline. It was obvious from the start that there were too many troops aboard, so the battalion waited in the harbor all day of the 20th for the transport commander to send us back to Camp Dix or Seaside Heights. But nobody was sent back. On the morning of the 21st the United States and the Statue of Liberty slipped quietly into the distance, as the ship headed out to sea on the wettest dry run the battalion had ever experienced. The food was good and the view was the same for many days.

. . . When we weren't shifting barracks bags, each man was dealt five cards and then put his meager savings into the center of the circle. We also lost some money on dice, and on betting where we were going to land, when the war was going to end, etc. It was on the ship that we first met the Japanese Americans of the 100th Infantry Battalion, with whom we were proud to serve in combat. They are tops on our list of well-disciplined and courageous troops — and they weren't slouches at those poker sessions.

Everyone who could fit on the deck slept there. Everyone else went down to the hole assigned to his ships' company — crawled over a pyramid of bodies and onto a shelf to which he was assigned . . . . Those who had the patience to wait in line ate two excellent meals each day. There was plenty of food — which was obvious to anyone who watched the vast amount of it going over the sides. But the trip was not at all rough. We were very lucky. For entertainment we had boat drills almost every day — Mae Wests and all. But nothing happened and we slid through the Straights of Gibraltar, said the appropriate things about the blueness of the Mediterranean, and continued heading toward Oran. We encountered no enemy action.

"Sailing Wailing"

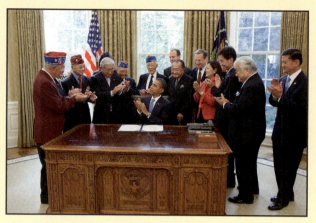
President Barack Obama and his guests applaud after signing S.1055, a bill to grant the Congressional Gold Medal, collectively, to the legendary 100th Japanese American Infantry Battalion, in recognition of their dedicated service during World War II. Also present are Rep. Mike Honda and Secretary of Veterans Affairs Eric Shinseki.

1943
100th Infantry soldiers receiving training in the use of grenades

When my parents moved to Ewa Beach on the island of Oahu in the 60's, they rented a wonderful old house overlooking the Pacific. My brothers - young boys - loved it there. They would often "skip school" when the surf was up and ride the waves for hours. The house was owned by Mr. Yoshioka, a Japanese-American who sometimes came by to check out his property on weekends.

I was visiting my family in April of 1989 - the month and year my father died - when I had the opportunity to meet Mr. Yoshioka, who remarked about the flower garden I was planting in the backyard. He asked about Dad - who was sitting outside most of the day recuperating from surgery, enjoying the sunshine and gentle breezes of the Pacific. Many people came by to visit with my father during those weeks. Mr. Yoshioka - for the first time - crossed the yard to say hello to Dad.

They discovered on that day that they both had been in WWII and boarded the same ship in 1943 - The SS Parker - which sailed to North Africa out of the port of Staten Island, NY. Mr. Yoshioka was with the legendary 100th Infantry, the Japanese-American troops who bravely fought for our country in WWII.

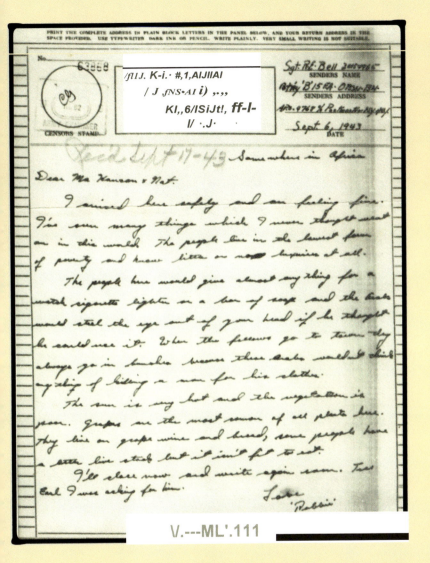

September 6, 1943
Sgt RE Bell
Battery B 15 Battery Observation Battalion

Somewhere in Africa

Dear Ma Hanson & Nat:

I arrived here safely and am feeling fine. I've seen many things which I never thought went on in this world. The people live in the lowest form of poverty and know little of luxuries at all.

The people here would give almost anything for a switch cigarette lighter or a bar of soap and the Arabs would steal the eye out of your head if he thought he could use it. When the fellows go to town they always go in bunches because these Arabs wouldn't think anything of killing a man for his clothes.

The sun is very hot and the vegetation is poor. Grapes are the most common of all plants here. They live on grape wine and bread, some people have a little live stock but it isn't fit to eat.

I'll close now and write again soon. Tell Earl I was asking for him.

Love, 'Robbie'

North Africa: Into the Fire

On 9/02/43 we left the battleship and steamed into Oran Harbor.

At Oran we learned to distrust all Army guide books. The females were unattractive and the population filthier than we had been led to expect. The natives could not understand a word of our polished Arabic. A weird assortment of humanity swarmed all over us with cries of "Seegareet, Joe?" or "Bon Bon?" Then we proceeded cigarette-less and bon-bon-less to the Fleures staging area, some 12 miles east of Oran. We stayed in Fleures for two weeks and then were ordered to Cape Falcon, a bit west of Oran, Algeria. During this stay in the Oran area, we became "oriented." The men learned how to control breathing while walking through the putrid air of an Arab community. They learned to drink foul water and also learned the difference between three-point-two beer and Arab vino.

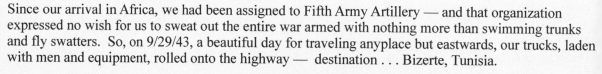

Complete with headsets and no overshoes, we sat in the sand and watched flies kick up dust and dirt for 24 hours a day — every day. We argued with military police in Oran and swam in the Mediterranean. We took long road marches in search of nonexistent oases, and we swatted and swallowed assorted African insects.

Since our arrival in Africa, we had been assigned to Fifth Army Artillery — and that organization expressed no wish for us to sweat out the entire war armed with nothing more than swimming trunks and fly swatters. So, on 9/29/43, a beautiful day for traveling anyplace but eastwards, our trucks, laden with men and equipment, rolled onto the highway — destination . . . Bizerte, Tunisia.

On the first night we were bivouacked near Orleansville, having covered 160 miles in the first leg of a nearly 900 mile journey. In the succeeding days we put Blida, El Hassie, and Souk Ahras behind us. Bizerte was a skeleton of a city, the first real ruin we saw. But we had been prepared for scenes of destruction by sights we had seen along Rommel's road of retreat. When we encamped just west of Bizerte, we were all tired and well satisfied with the successful completion of a major truck movement. Of the trip itself not much can be said — Africa had more beauty than we expected — more hills, more fertile valleys, more C-rations, and more Arabs popping up in the most desolate places.

As the mud got deeper and the rain got wetter, we began to think we were preparing for three more months of African maneuvers. But on the morning of October 21 we received the order to "crank up," so we struck tents for the last time on African soil and sailed from Bizerte without regrets. The prevailing feeling was that no other land on earth could duplicate the dust, the heat, the flies, and the barrenness of North Africa.

Chapter II: Road To Rome
Salerno, Naples, Volturno, Cassino, Anzio, Rome

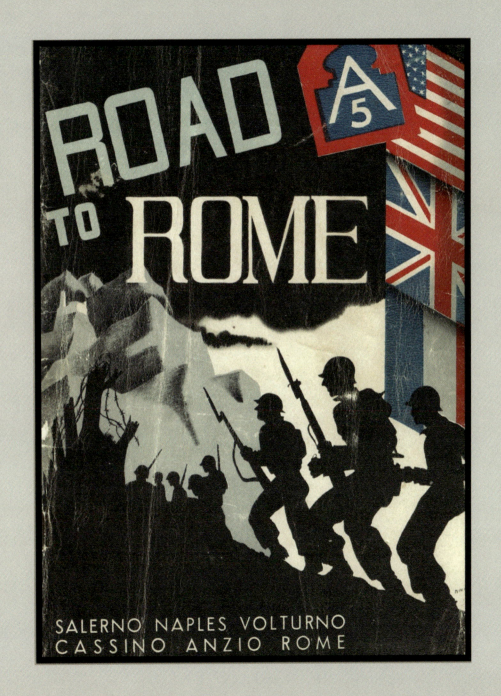

Dad used a black marker to outline the path that his troops followed as they pushed north through Italy. . .

Prologue - the Fifth Army

On September 9, 1943, the quiet beaches of Paestum and Salerno broke into a hell of tracers, flares, and shells. This was the battle baptism of General Mark Clark's Fifth Army and British General Montgomery's Eighth Army. It was the first stop on the road to Rome.

The last stop was taken on the morning of 4 June 1944 when American troops of the Fifth Army entered the world's most historic city — ROME — the capital of Italy.

The American troops of the Fifth Army were the first of their country's forces to invade the European fortress. They belonged to the first American Army to be activated on foreign soil in WWII and they freed the first Axis capital.

* * *

The Italian campaign of WWII was the most destructive fought in Europe - a long, bitter and highly attritional conflict that raged up the country's mountainous leg of blasted landscapes, rain and mud, and months on end with the front line barely moving.

Frontline troops casualty rates at Cassino and Anzio, along the notorious Gothic Line, were as high as they had been on the Western Front in the First World War.

The line up of Fifth Army troops set the stage for the capture of Naples while other units farther inland could continue to press the enemy back toward the Volturno River. Nearly all bridges over the river were blown up by the Germans — mines and booby traps were placed where our resourceful enemy anticipated routes in advance. Following the destruction of the bridges they then covered crossing sites with fire. The Fifth Army infantry was deployed, climbing steep-sided mountains. As they moved across the difficult terrain, they flanked and fought and flanked and fought again. Soldiers and mules lugged food and ammunitions over hazardous mountain trails on dark, rain-swept nights. The Fifth was unique in that it had a truly international profile. In addition to American white troops and black troops, the army included British, French, Italian, Algerian, Moroccan, Polish, New Zealander, Australian and Canadian forces.

Dad loved the people of Italy who opened their doors, their hearts and their hearths to the American soldiers. He came home from the war with a surprising knowledge of both the language and the food. He actually studied Italian in Florence at the end of the war. We loved finding him in our kitchen creating wonderful sauces, meatballs, sausages, lasagna, polenta, ravioli. A family favorite was his special pizza with fresh tomatoes made with homemade dough on a large rectangular cookie sheet. The Bell kids fought for every piece. We surprised him one Christmas with a pasta machine made in Italy so he could make his own pasta.

The Capture of Naples
October 1943

By nightfall of 30 Sept, the red glow of Vesuvius shed its radiance on the Fifth Army. Forces were poised to enter Naples. Allied bombing had damaged the harbor installations of this famous port city.

Dad's unit sailed directly from Africa into the port of Naples on October 23, 1943 — bypassing Sicily and Salerno. The Fifth army needed the port of Naples as an entry point for the supplies and troops necessary to carry on a major campaign. The Germans were determined to hold Naples long enough to destroy as much of the harbor and utilities systems as possible. German demolitions and destruction had taken a heavy toll . . . the enemy had unleashed its full fury of wrath.

Ratt-lerry rigs like this played a useful part in crossing the Volturno.

The most decorated soldier of WWll, Audie Murphy, 3rd 'Division, was Great uncle to our Grandchildren, John David and Virginia Head.

Dad and Audie fought together at Anzio and crossed the Volturno River on the Road to Rome.

The Fifth Army at Anzio
January 1944 - Landing at Anzio. Operation Shingle ...

In the winter of 1943-44, Anzio, a small Mediterranean resort and port some thirty-five miles south of Rome, played a crucial role in the fortunes of World War II as the target of an amphibious Allied landing. The Allies planned to bypass the strong German defenses along the Gustav Line and at Monte Cassino sixty miles to the southeast, which were holding up the American and British armies and preventing the liberation of Rome.

By taking advantage of allied command of the sea and air to effect complete surprise, infantry and armored forces landed at Anzio on January 22, 1944. The expectation was that they would secure the beachhead and then push inland to cut off the two main highways and railroads supplying the German forces to the south, either trapping and annihilating the German armies or forcing them to withdraw to the north, thus opening the way to Rome.

But the reality of one of the most desperate campaigns of World War II was bad management, external meddling, poorly relayed orders, and uncertain leadership. The Anzio beachhead became a deathtrap with allied troops forced to fight for their lives for four dreadful months. The eventual victory in Italy in May 1944 was muted, bitter, and overshadowed by the allied landings in Normandy on June 6 ...

A unknown solder's story at Anzio:

"I guess those first few minutes in combat are to say the most life changing - a lot of us just stood there in terror. I remember a British officer screaming at us. 'What's the matter with you blokes, do you wanna live always!' as he grabbed me and we jumped in a basement for cover.

An incident that I remember vividly . . . We had been sleeping in that farmhouse and Wallace Chapman and I drifted off upstairs to write a letter home. As we were writing, a shell hit across the road — about 150 feet from the farmhouse. Another one followed, that one landing right beside the house. We dropped what we were doing and ran like madmen. As we reached the outside, a shell hit the house and knocked an entire wall out. We went on around to the front. Wallace had made a right turn to try and make it to the nearby stable. Again, with the guidance of the Lord, I ran back toward the house and got behind an old car. A lieutenant was screaming to get the hell out — one at a time we ran across the yard. When it came my time, I took off as fast as I could and tripped over a grape vine. When I hit the ground, a shell hit behind me and covered me with dirt . . . In a ten-minute span, I was saved twice! It was shocking to see Wallace dead who had just been writing a letter a few minutes before . . . I sent home the letter Wallace was writing; he didn't get to finish it. I hope his family found some comfort in that. Eight of my comrades were killed in that stable."

I remember Dad and his war buddy, Hank Williams, telling a story at the Jersey Shore where our families vacationed together in the summer of 1980:

```
...  They were hiding in a barn together when a bomb came through the roof blowing off an
entire wall. Dad and Hank were hiding in the hay on the other side. They both chuckled at
their good fortune - a little glassy eyed - as they told this harrowing story.
```

Excerpt from Stars and Stripes:
After Jerry's all outpush, the Anzio campaign resolved itself into a stalemate. For over three months we sat there and growled at each other. We sincerely hoped that the growling disconcerted the Krauts as much as it did us. The stalemate found us in another wooded area about 2 kilometers south of Padigliona. Draft shells found us there too, so we set to work digging our elaborate dugouts. Everyone lived underground. Days were spent on improvement of underground position ... shelves were carved into the earthen walls and snake entrances had to be continually plugged up - if they wanted to come in they had to use the same hole we did. Rags and blankets were draped around the walls to make the place cozy and lighting systems had to be devised. Each man had about a half mile of wire strung around a rusty razor blade for the popular version of the 'fox hole radio' invented at Anzio ... if you listened carefully, you might imagine you were hearing a radio program.

By the time we got off the beachhead, we all looked jaundiced because of lack of sunlight - those dugouts felt that good. Only on occasion would we emerge for a game of softball in the open field across the road where the medical tent was located. This practice was discontinued when the medical command car was blown sky high by a shell that was coming towards home plate. So we all crawled back into our holes and sulked.

The longer we stayed on the Beachhead, the longer grew our casualty lists. Each of us left a little bit of ourselves at Anzio and the months spent on the Beachhead shall always live in our memories. Let us never forget the comrades we left there.

The Beachhead was stirring and the fight for Rome was on. As the infantry advanced, we followed as close as we could. Down the purple path and up the railroad bed we tramped with rod, tape, and transit. The first days after we had left the accustomed security of our dugouts, sleeping on the ground was done with a sense of utter nakedness, especially when Jerry planes buzzed overhead.

Heading to Rome - Crossing the Volturno

On the night of October 11, 1943 a patrol set out to probe the river for a crossing point. The weather was cold and rainy. Cautiously, the men waded into the swollen Volturno river. The water was chest-deep, the current swift. Baffled at one point, the patrol tried another point of entry — all this in pitch blackness . . . Darkness gave way to a full moon. The enemy was aware of the usual routine activity on our side of the river.

At 2000 hours, enemy troops must have been jolted by the simultaneous artillery concentrations that fell on them . . . Canadians and Americans captured Mt. La Difensa and a regiment of the 36th Infantry Division captured Mt. Maggiore. There was bitter fighting in the worst kind of weather and terrain. It taxed the endurance of every soldier climbing, fighting, and maneuvering in rainswept valleys and sleet-lashed mountains.

Dad's Story to Michael:
He was somewhere in the mountains. The men camped down for the night and in the morning Dad went off into the bushes to relieve himself. He looked up and saw someone on the other side, doing the same thing. They made eye contact and stood there frozen staring at each other. Dad was scared and he figured the German soldier was too. But rather than pulling their guns on each other, they both backed away and as soon as they got a few yards apart, they ran for their lives in opposite directions. No bullets fired. Just two scared young guys who didn't want to shoot anyone.

Dad told this story with flare, as he did, and made it into a joke, as he did. But I always remember the story and made him tell it over and over again.

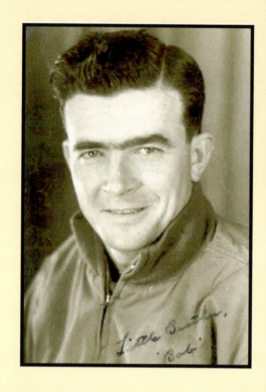

Men lived for days on snowy mountain peaks. They stayed there to repel counterattacks and to inch forward when possible, existing in the crudest of shelters suffering from fatigue and exposure as they continued to fight. Our movement was often confined to the hours of darkness and in that icy blackness mule trains were led up the mountains. When even the mules couldn't negotiate such terrains, our soldiers shouldered pack-boards and portered ammunition and supplies.

The last step on the Road to Rome was taken on the morning of June 4, 1944, when American troops of the Fifth Army entered the world's most historic city — ROME — the capital of Italy.

December 4, 1943 Sgt RE Bell
Batt'y "B" 15 FA Obsn Bn
Italy

Dear Ma Hanson & Nat,

I just got another package from you. It just said Christmas Package on the outside so maybe that was #1. I guess I'm doing as good here as I would at home. It sure makes a guy feel good to get packages like that. I'm never very good at expressing my appreciation because I appreciate things so much I just don't know what to say or write so I just say thanks. Its about the same around here except its a little noisier lately. If you read the latest news you'll know just about where I am and how things are here. I received your letters and journals. Well, I'll close now hoping you are both OK and not getting worn out while Christmas shopping.

                Love, your son-in-law, 'Robbie'

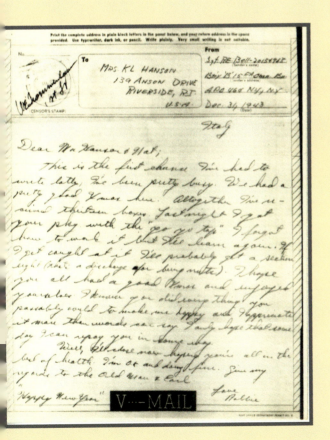

December 31, 1943 Sgt RE Bell - 20154965
Batt'y "B" 15 FA Obsn Bn
APO 464 NY, NY
Italy

Dear Ma Hanson & Nat,

This is the first chance I've had to write lately. I've been pretty busy. We had a pretty good Christmas here. Altogether I've received thirteen boxes. Last night I got your package with the "yo yo top." I forgot how to work it but I'll learn again. If I get caught at it I'll probably get a section eight (that's a discharge for being nuts).

I hope you all had a good Xmas and enjoyed yourselves. I know you did everything you possibly could to make me happy and I appreciate it more than words can say. I only hope that some day I can repay you in some way.

Well, I'll close now hoping you are all in the best of health. I'm OK and doing fine. Give my regards to the Old Man & Earl.

"Happy New Year."

                Love, 'Robbie'

A postcard that dad saved of a wedding somewhere in Italy.

Dad wrote on the back of the postcard:

I'd like to get to see one of these weddings. The people here always travel like this. They can't drive cars in most places. They still have the weddings like this one

Grass shacks - in Italy!

Anzio Beach
Dad is back, center

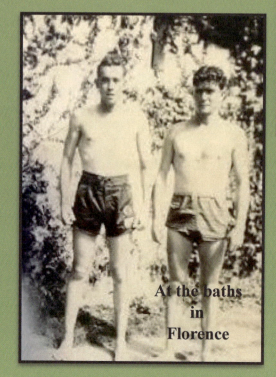

At the baths in Florence

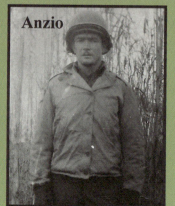

Anzio

ABOUT HANK WILLIAMS

He was without a doubt Dad's best friend.
His brother throughout the war. His brother after the war.

Soon after the war, Hank and his wife Peg drove from NJ to our lake cabin in RI one summer day - My 4 year old sister Bonnie and I watched fascinated as they walked up the hill. Peg looked like a movie star - blonde curls, bright red lips, and high heel shoes. Wow! On her arm was her man Hank - bigger than life. I mean a seriously big guy. Bonnie said that he was bigger than the giant turtle at our local county fair.

In this photo of Dad and Hank in Italy, Dad said that Hank was standing on the top step.
Hank sure was the soldier to have by your side in Italy in WWII. They were never separated throughout the war as far as I know.

Our childhood always included visits to Peg and Hank's. And most every summer they returned to our lake house. He was wonderful; soft spoken and kind. Until the age of 12, I thought he was my real blood uncle. I remember one of our visits to NJ. Hank took us all to Atlantic City. where we walked the famous boardwalk - took a ride in a wooden rickshaw - with all the taffy and cotton candy I could possibly eat. Watched the horse jump off the famous steel pier into the surf. Went underwater in a glass cage to the ocean floor. Scary but exciting.

They visited us often - mostly in the summer. Dad and Hank worked on the cabin doing projects like building a back porch and making bunk beds for Bonnie and me out of birch trees.

Hank quickly became a real blood brother to Dad's family - hanging out with my father's 3 brothers - all safely home from the war - as they worked on the family boats - priming and painting - or repairing a roof or building a shed. Always fun. Happy days. Quahauging and fishing. Eating steamers. And of course, there was the cold beer. Probably Narragansett. I remember them lugging in barrels and setting them up next to the shed. Those Bell boys sure could drink. And Hank too.

Dad told me a story about three soldiers at the end of the war walking back to headquarters to celebrate victory in Italy and receive their orders to go home. He said that they kept changing places as they walked the dusty road together, so happy to be going home. One of them - the soldier in the middle - stepped on a land mine which killed him. I'm certain that Dad lived with the memory of that horror all of his life. What I also know for certain is that it wasn't Dad and it wasn't Hank who stepped on the land mine that day. They made it down that dusty road together. They went home.

Hank Williams was at that last reunion in Akron Ohio in 1990. I sat next to him and fell asleep on his shoulder. That's the kind of guy he was. Lovely.

Feb 11, 1944
Somewhere in Italy

Dear Ma Hanson and Nat,

First of all congratulations, Nat and Earl. I don't suppose it will be long now. This is the first chance I've had to write you in quite a while. Gin will tell you why or maybe you have an idea why yourself. I got all your valentines and would never have known there was such a day if it wasn't for you folks and Gin (and Maureen). By Gin's letters I guess you all had a pretty good Christmas, considering the circumstances. I only hope that next year the war will be over and everybody will be home again.

You wrote and asked me to send you a request letter. I did send one to Gin and she said what I wanted was on the way. I can't think of anything else I need or want to request for except maybe a good dish of speggetti and meatballs. Thanks a lot for asking me and if I need anything I'll write to you. I wonder if you could wrap up Gin and Maureen and send them to me). I'll close now hoping you are in the best of health.

Say hello to Earl and the Old Man for me.
Love 'Robbie'

Sgt RE Bell
Batt'y "B" 15 FA Obsn Bn March 11, 1944

Anzio Beachhead

Dear Ma Hanson & Nat,
I haven't been able to write much lately; I've received all your letters on the bank business and I will write to Mr. Underwood and get it all straight as soon as I can. I want to thank you for all the trouble you went through. It sure is a mess.

You've probably read in the papers all about this place where I am now. It gets plenty hot here at times and it isn't from the weather. We all dig our holes deeper and better here and I'd like to thank the guy who invented "fox holes."

I received a pkg. from Gin with all the soups and other things I asked for. Boy, that soup really hits the spot especially when you've been eating 'C' rations for a couple of weeks. When I finish this I'm going to get a hair cut (the first one in almost 3 months). I'll close now and will write again soon.

Love to all 'Robbie'

The Fifth Army at Monte Cassino

The Cold Italian Winter of 1943–44 . . . Germany would lose the war, but they still held much of Italy, leaving the Allies to fight their way north to capture Rome—a route no army had taken since Hannibal traversed the Alps to avoid it. Overlooking the only possible passage stood the ancient Abbey of Monte Cassino. The ultimate decision to bomb Monte Cassino was one of the most controversial—and tragic—events of World War II. The combat that followed was just as tragic: Soldiers from more than a dozen nations fought through that savage winter in a ferocious battle that allowed no advance or retreat. This was an epic tale of men—and monks—at war.

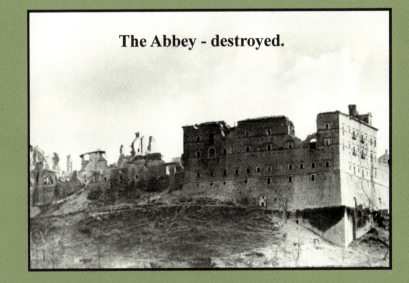

The Abbey - destroyed.

The Abbey, rebuilt after the war.

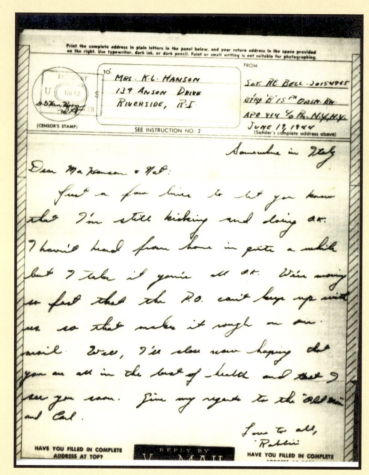

Sgt RE Bell
Batt'y "B" 15 FA Obsn Bn
Somewhere in Italy

June 19, 1944

Dear Ma Hanson & Nat,

First a few lines to let you know that I'm still kicking and doing O.K. I haven't heard from home in quite a while but I take it you're all O.K. We are moving so fast that the P.O. can't keep up with us so that makes it rough on our mail.

Well, I'll close now hoping that you are all in the best of health and that I see you soon. Give my regards to the "Old Man" and Earl.

                                            Love to all,
                                            'Robbie'

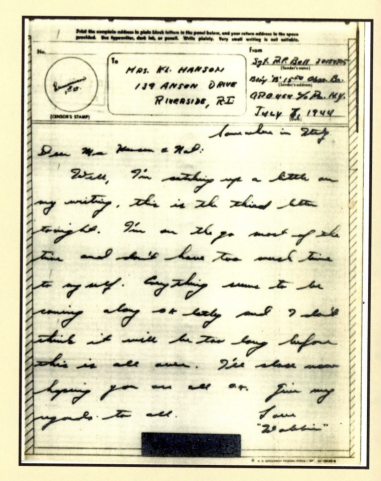

July 8, 1944
Somewhere in Italy

Dear Ma Hanson & Nat,

Well, I'm catching up a little on my writing. This is the third letter tonight. I'm on the go most of the time and don't have too much time to myself. Every thing seems to be coming along ok lately and I don't think it will be too long before this is all over. I'll close now hoping you are all ok. Give my regards to all.

                                          Love, 'Robbie'

General Mark Clark's Victory Message to the Fifth Army troops

The American troops of the Fifth Army were the first of their country's forces to invade the European fortress. They belonged to the first American army to be activated on foreign soil in WWII and they freed the first Axis capital.

The delivery of Rome came with special feelings of pride. You did what no other army ever did. You attacked from the south, expelled the foe, and entered Rome.

Behind you lay nine months of campaign. Each foot of the way to Rome is a tribute to your courage and to your indomitable will to win. In Rome, your feet trod upon ground that answered to the soft tread of sandals worn by tribesmen six centuries before Christ. You passed the ruins of a civilization that flourished two thousand years before your own country was discovered. A campaign like this one can only be adequately covered in many volumes . . . The unknown soldier who removed a mine, who drove a truck, who evacuated the wounded man from the heights of Mt. Sammucro, or the united soldiers that repaired a bridge, unloaded a cargo ship, or hauled supplies . . . They all played a vital part in the triumph of June 1944.

Rome is free. You made it so. But Rome is merely one symbolic objective. Only with the complete defeat of the Axis powers can we rest upon our arms and feel that our job is done.

~ General Mark Clark

General Clark is shown entering Rome with his Chief of Staff, Major General Alfred M. Gruenther (left rear) and the Rome Area Commander, Major General Harry H. Johnson. St. Peter's looms in the background.

Past the historic Colosseum, Fifth Army infantry marches through Rome in pursuit of the fleeing Germans.

Liberated by Fifth Army from long years of Axis tyranny, the people of Rome greeted the troops with an emotional enthusiasm that defies description.

"With God's help, we shall carry on the task which they began."
General Clark, Memorial Day, Anzio.

To the Officers and Men of the Fifth Army:

You have made this story. It is compounded of the snow and sleet of the Apennines, the tenacious mud of the mountain valley, the heat of summer in a foreign land, and the cold of winter. It is written in the blood of your comrades, bound in the imperishable glory of their memory. You have fought long and hard, but you have won a memorable victory.

I am proud of having been one of you. No general has ever commanded a finer army.

I think no general ever will.

L. K. Truscott, Jr.
Lieutenant General,
U.S. Army Commanding

Chapter III: 19 Days
From the Apennines to the Alps

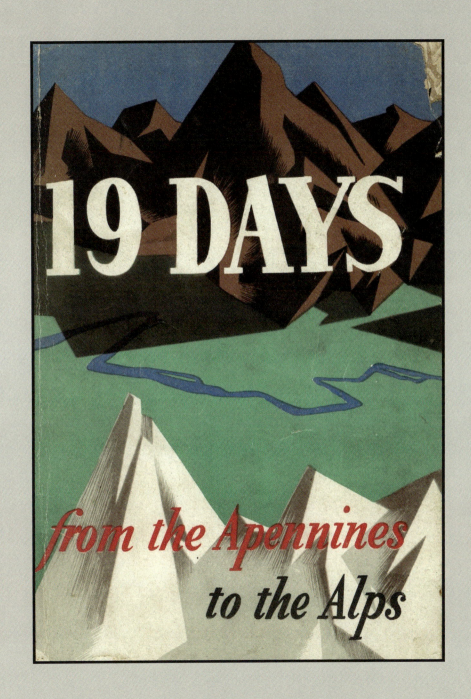

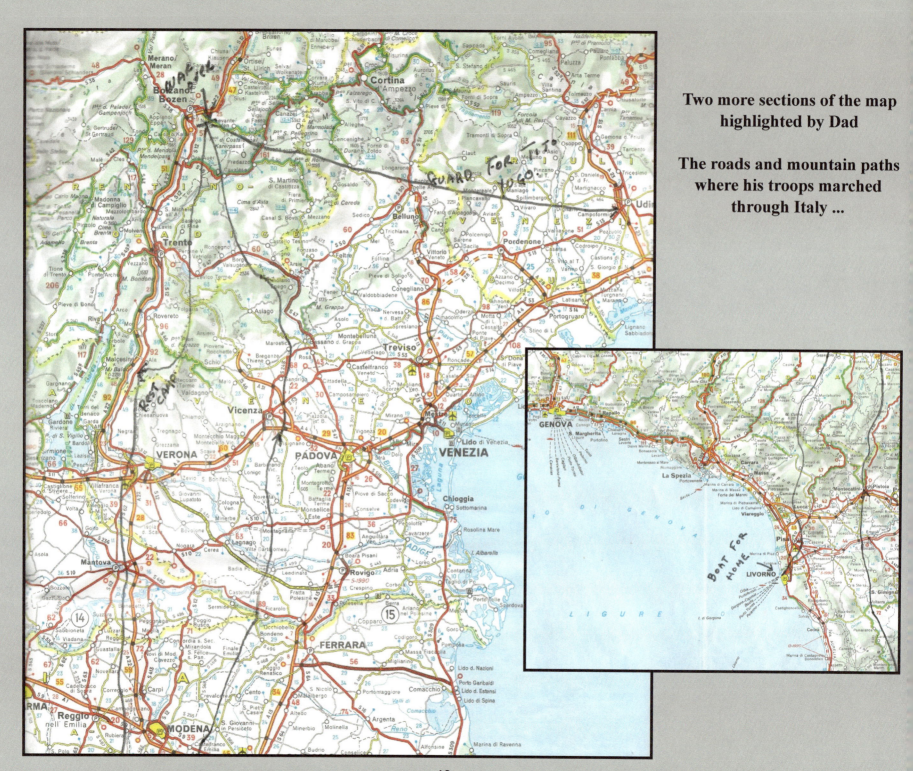

Two more sections of the map highlighted by Dad

The roads and mountain paths where his troops marched through Italy ...

The Po Valley - April and May 1945

.... So it developed all over the Po Valley during those tremendous days. You had to see it to believe it, and even then you weren't sure. The Fifth Army had come down out of the Apennines with such a rush and in such concentrated strength that the enemy was unable to organize his intermediate defensive positions south of the Po. There was plenty of hard fighting, but more and more the battle took on the aspect of a chase, a gigantic mopping-up operation. The wounded waited in their pain to be evacuated by litter bearers who took hours to descend the mountains with their burdens. Men suffered from trench foot and all the hardships of mountain warfare.

.... Men, women, plump young girls, and small children lined the highway and the village streets, screaming "Evviva!" and "Ciao" and tossed spring flowers into the vehicles. Our men could take it. They were tough. Besides, why get all worked up over a dream? They'd wake up in the morning and they'd still be up there in those mountains with krauts looking down at them. This level land, this slick paved road couldn't be true. Presently one of them believed it. Standing up suddenly in the truck, he yelled "whoopee!" blew a kiss at a blonde girl and abruptly sat down again.

The German forces had been virtually self-sustaining in the rich valley of the Po. What our troops had come to call the "Promised Land" was indeed a "land of milk and honey" — to say nothing of wheat and rice and fruit and livestock. While southern Italy lived on semi-starvation rations, the Po Valley residents had all they needed and more, lacking only tobacco, sugar, and a few other luxuries. The krauts had all they could eat, but because of the destruction of their oil plants, and with railroad and highway bridges out, movement to and from Germany had become a tedious and hazardous process, and they were not able to loot the country as thoroughly as they had done in Denmark and the low countries.

Happy citizens lined the streets as troops and Partisans paraded.

The Mountain Division attacked Monte Belvedere and the enemy held positions along Highway 64. It was here that the army spring offensive was later to begin. The fresh mountain troops trained to razor-edge fineness but as yet lacking extensive combat experience, were assigned the task of clearing commanding heights held by the Germans.

With a verve and enthusiasm reflecting their caliber and training, our men took the Serrrasiccia- Campiano Ridge, Monte Belvedere and Monte Torraccia, and continued on to the northeast. The British forces kept pace with the US forces as it spearheaded the attack. After 16 days, General Truscott called a halt. This was the position of the

Fifth Army at the beginning of April 1945 as it prepared for the push that was to culminate in complete victory in Italy.

Men and mules plodded through the mud of Appennine Trails.

`I will always remember the reunion of the 15th Field Artillery Observation Battalion in Akron, Ohio in 1990 - a year after Dad died. Mom and I flew to Akron together. This would be Mom's last reunion - the first time without my Dad. I honestly never thought about how sad this must have been for her. Mom never showed tears - only her signature hearty laughter. She was a very tough lady. The women in our family can only hope to have inherited her courage.`

`So much joy among the remaining brothers to be together again. Lots of stories into the wee hours. One was about my dad, their missing comrade, whom they fondly tag-named 'Sgt. Ding-Dong.'`

`There was a terrifying blast in the night. Jumping out of their fox holes, armed with rifles, into the pitch blackness, the men searched for the enemy. What they discovered instead was Bob Bell's whiskey barrel hidden in the brush. It had exploded!`

"F'ire for effect." "Ceaso firing. Mission accomplished." Fifth Army artil'lery smashes another German bridge.

Enemy motor transport suffered from lack of spare parts and shortage of fuel. Our air force had made almost a no-man's land of the entire Po Valley. Vehicles and trains moved in daylight only at great risk. There were no longer any bridges over the Po River and all supplies had to be ferried. Even at night, movement over the roads in the Po Valley was hazardous because of the operations of our night bombers.

It was estimated that the enemy had on hand 14 days of supplies, while he still had control of the great industrial regions of the northwest, including the factory cities of Milan and Turin, with their automobile and airplane plants. In preparation perhaps for the development of Hitler's National Redoubt* in the Bavarian Alps, he had moved large numbers of drill presses, lathes, and other machine tools from these cities into the highway tunnels on the western shore of Lake Garda. Here, securely sheltered, they were turning out airplane engines. Hitler, from his shelter on Wilheimstrasse, had announced to the world that the German armies would fight to the last man.

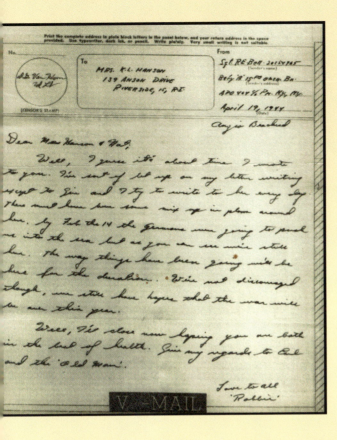

April 19, 1944 Anzio Beachhead

Dear Ma Hanson & Nat

Well, I guess it's about time I wrote to you. I've sort of let up on my letter writing except to Gin and I try to write to her every day.

There must have been some mix up in plans around here. By Feb the 14 the Germans were going to push us into the sea but as you can see we're still here. The way things have been going we'll be here for the duration. We're not discouraged though, we still have hopes that the war will be over this year.

Well, I'll close now hoping you are both in the best of health. Give my regards to Earl and the "Old Man."

Love to all, 'Robbie'

No date [May 1944]
Italy

Dear Ma Hanson,

I guess its about time I did a little writing. I don't think I've written more than three letters in the last two weeks. You probably know about where I am by the news. It has been a long time since we've moved as fast as we're moving now, but in a way it's good to be on the go again. The Germans are just about finished here and I don't think it will be too long and they will be finished all over. The Partisans did a good job on Mussolini and his gang, but I don't think that Hitler is dead, although I hope so.

Well, I guess that's about all for now, so I'll close wishing you a very happy Mother's Day and hoping that it won't be long until I see you again.

Love, 'Robbie'

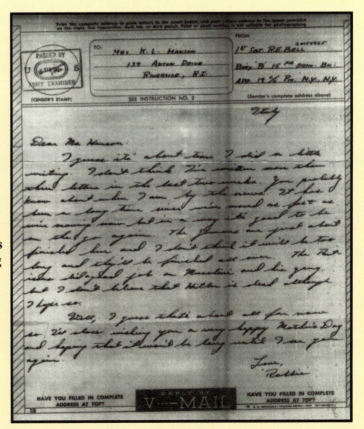

The Finale

On the right flank of the Fifth Army's front — hardly a "front" now — the 91st fought several fire fights on the way to Bassano, and the 88th hit fanatical resistance in Vicenza where bazookas knocked out nine of our tanks. The 88th continued to push on to cross the Astico River.

In the next two days, the Fifth Army had strong columns on main highways to the northwest, north, and northeast. One spearhead had reached the Swiss frontier and was fanning out along the border, another had turned northeast from the top of Garda toward Trento and the Brenner. The 84th was west of Vicenza. The 88th, after pushing northeast, crossed the Brenta River north of Padua and captured Bassano (Mike, Lisa, and I visited Bassano del Grappa in September 2014).

At the end of April in the Ligurian sector, the 34th division captured in mass the 75th German Army Corps comprised of some 40,000 Germans. The First armored was spread out along the Ticino River and regiments were guarding the roads to France. Partisans had taken Milan and had caught and executed Mussolini. The death of Benito Mussolini, the deposed Italian fascist dictator, occurred on 28 April 1945, in the final days of World War II, when he was summarily executed by Italian Communists in the small village of Giulino di Mezzegra in northern Italy.

The road up the east shore of Lake Garda is in many places only a scratch along the cliffs passing through several tunnels (Mike, Lisa, and I traveled that winding road — white knuckled in 2014). The mountain infantry was met by seemingly impassable road blocks, with cliffs towering hundreds of feet high on the left and the lake hundreds of feet deep below.

Milan - Mussolini and executed fascists

Here they found blown out tunnels and bridges, all artfully covered by 88's and machines concealed in tunnels and caves. Two amphibious landings were made that outflanked the roadblocks and opened the way for the engineers to repair the damage. The enemy fought back viciously and two Dukws (amphibious trucks) were sunk and still lie in hundreds of feet of blue water with their priceless cargo on the bottom of Lake Garda. A small group crossed the lake in Dukws and raided Mussolini's villa at Gargagnano capturing valuable documents but not Mussolini, who was then hanging dead in Milan . . . .

To exertions seemingly beyond human endurance, days and nights felt momentarily lost, as if an intolerable silence had fallen; as if, indeed, soldiers had suddenly precipitated into a vacuum. Yet, they had known that something must happen . . . and soon. Whole divisions and corps of the German and Italian Fascists had been surrendering. There was no longer a German line, no longer an organized defense — only a breakneck race to the mountains and the sea. Men were too weary to think. The thoughts of thousands of our infantry were clearly expressed by one motorman with the 88th Division who, with astonishment in his voice, sat on the ground and murmured, "Thank God I made it!"

The Germans, cut to ribbons, had no choice but to surrender. The German surrender, the largest-scale capitulations so far in the war, was to have a tremendous affect on the conclusion of hostilities throughout Europe, less than a week later. It knocked a million German soldiers out of the war and provided the moral impetus for the collapse of the Nazis everywhere. It laid the foundation for the return of peace in Europe.

At the close of the campaign nearly half of Italy, an area with a population of some 23 million people, was under direct control of the Fifth Army. Such complex problems as . . .
- the movement of hundreds of thousands of refugees and displaced persons;
- the disarming of the Partisans, from whom approximately 200,000 weapons were collected;
- the care and transportation of some of Italy's greatest works of art which had been retrieved from the Germans;
- the feeding of the entire civilian population in the area;
- the administration of justice;
- tnd the supply of civilian labor to the army

. . . were but a few of the manifold civilian tasks which had to be undertaken. These were accomplished successfully and concurrently with the progress of military operations and kept pace at all times with the rapidly moving situation.

From the Straits of Messina to the Brenner Pass, Italy was free. The last great battle of the war in the Mediterranean Theater had been fought and won. The Fifth Army, born overseas, was victorious.

Epilogue
The British Eighth and the American Fifth Armies had reached the end of the long, long roads from El Alamen, Salerno, and Naples. They had destroyed the enemy in Italy, and in doing so, had demonstrated to the world the power of coordinated action by united nations. Magnificently equipped and sustained by the untiring efforts and support of the homefront, the 15th Army — that polyglot group of many nationalities fighting as a unit for a single cause — had done its share, and perhaps more, in the fight for human liberty.

They made it . . . in 19 days!!

Italy
August 2, 1944

Dear Ma Hanson & Nat,

I'm an early bird this morning, this is my second letter. I just got through writing to Gin. I'm writing this letter to ask you if you would send me some chewing gum. I don't get much of it here and there is no place to buy it. If so I would appreciate if you could do it.

I wrote a letter to Agnes and Dwight so now I don't owe anyone except Madame and I'll do that within the next few days. Well I guess that's about all for now so I'll close hoping to see you all soon.

          Love to All,
          'Robbie'

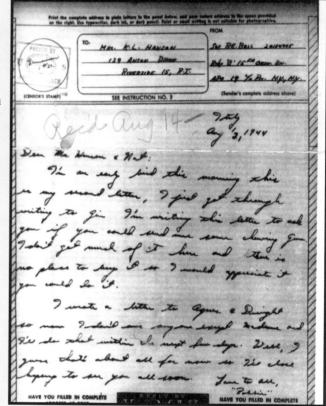

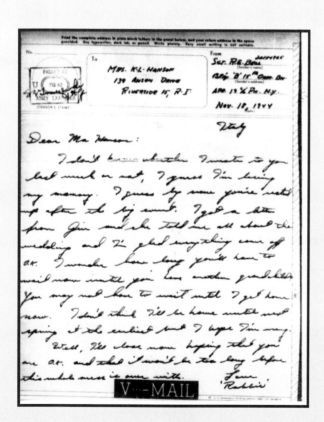

Nov 18, 1944
Italy

Dear Ma Hanson:

I don't know whether I wrote to you last week or not, I guess I'm losing my memory. I guess by now you're rested up after the big event. I got a letter from Gin and she told me all about the wedding and I'm glad that everything came off OK. I wonder how long you'll have to wait now until you have another grandchild. You may not have to wait until I get home now. I don't think I'll be home till next spring at the earliest but I hope I'm wrong.

Well, I'll close now hoping that you are OK and that it won't be too long before before this whole mess is over with.

          Love,
          'Robbie'

Chapter IV: Walking In His Boots
Trip to Italy 2014

Maureen and Michael
Sienna

Michael's Story

One of the many highlights of our trip to Italy was a visit to Bassano del Grappa - a town not so far from Lake Garda that was one of Dad's favorites. He loved that region and we could see why - it's so unbelievably beautiful! Looking at the postcard which was found in "the box," it is apparent that his battalion was encamped at this beautiful villa for a few days - or perhaps even longer.

On the back of the postcard in Dad's handwriting was "We stayed here". So, of course, while touring Italy in September of 2014, we were determined to find The Villa. When we stopped for lunch in Bassano along the River Brenta over the famous Ponte degli Alpini bridge, we asked various locals to direct us to the Villa – showing them the postcard. The response was "I've never heard of it . . . never seen it . . . It's not located in Bassagno." Maureen insisted that it must still be there – no one would tear it down - it was only 70 years ago - not so old in Italy.

A postcard from Dad during the war.

On back: *"We are staying in this building at present"*

So we drove to the City Information Center. Lisa and Maureen went inside while I stayed with the car. They were gone for quite a while. The response to their inquiry was disappointing: "No, it's not on any records that we can find." There was one staff member very determined to locate the Villa. She made several calls to tourism agencies throughout the region. And then - as luck will have it - just as the office was about to close for the day, the phone rang. "Wait!" she said excitedly, "I think we found the location!" She gave them a map and put an X on the area where she thought the Villa was located. The girls came out ecstatic! And we took off excitedly in the car to find it.

We got to the spot marked "X" but saw nothing that looked like the Villa - just a new highway and some other buildings. I had to turn around to head back; and when I did, we saw a street sign - Via Torricelli. Ah Ha! We headed down the old road - barely visible covered by tall weeds - then came to a private villa that was walled in with huge hedges. We stopped at the gate and looked in. The roofs had changed, but we knew it was it. The mountain in the background matched exactly with the post card. So Cool! Really made this a special trip. Of course, we celebrated with a bottle of good Italian wine.

Salute!
~ Mike

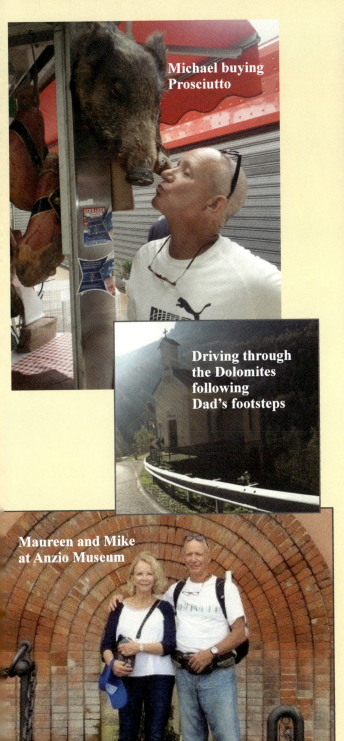
Michael buying Prosciutto

Driving through the Dolomites following Dad's footsteps

Maureen and Mike at Anzio Museum

Lisa in Bologna

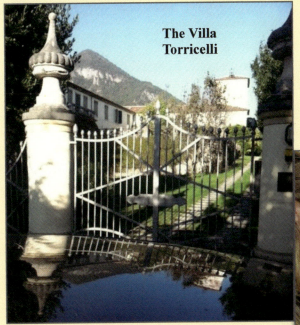
The Villa Torricelli

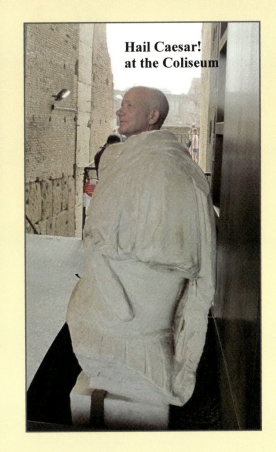
Hail Caesar! at the Coliseum

WAKIKI BEACH, 1968

Dad with Dan and Mike

Chapter V: The Bell Family

HONORING OUR FAMILY'S MILITARY

Parents

Margaret "Maggie" Molloy
&
Walter "Pop" Bell

Walter Francis Bell Jr.
US Navy
Quonset, Rhode Island

William James Bell
US Navy
The Pacific Theater

Robert Edward Bell
US Army
The European Theater

John Joseph Bell
US Navy
The Pacific Theater

The Riverside Kids

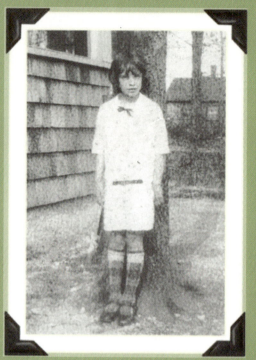

Mom - Age 9

Virginia Hanson was fun; a popular girl in the Riverside summer "gang". She was adventurous and a natural athlete who would dare all the boys to follow her as she swam across the river through the spinning whirlpool. Dangerous of course - but that's what made it exciting. One of those boys was Robbie Bell. She told me that she was attracted to his Irish good looks. He was a handsome guy for sure, with dark curly hair and bright blue eyes.

Then one summer evening destiny intervened when Robbie borrowed the family car and arranged a double date to impress a pretty girl named Ethel Crowther. That double date would include Ginnie Hanson and Billy Sweeney in the back seat. Dad's plan backfired when Ginnie beat Ethel to the front seat of the old Ford and sat down right next to him - where she belonged. Forever. Mom and Dad were married in 1940. They had a child [me] and a couple of years later Dad was off to Africa and Italy and WWII.

Destiny intervened a year later when Ethel Crowther and Billy Sweeney married. The two couples remained close friends throughout their lives. My Dad made it to 70 years. Sadly, Ethel died a couple of years before Dad. A few years after my Dad was gone, Bill Sweeney got on a plane from the west coast and flew to Jensen Beach Florida to ask my mother to marry him.

She did not marry Bill. I would imagine that she had had enough heartache for a lifetime after losing my Dad. I think it would have been comforting for Bill and Mom to be together. But that did not happen. I love this story. No one could have been more of a gentleman to want to take care of my mother than Bill Sweeney.

PS: In 2010 my brother Michael poured Mom's ashes into the river at Riverside. We all watched in sadness and amazement as her ashes rushed out to the location of the whirlpool..

Mom & Dad camping in Maine - 1939

The 30's and 40's

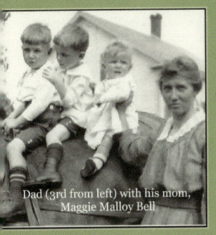
Dad (3rd from left) with his mom, Maggie Malloy Bell

Dad Age 11

Virginia, her sister, Natalie, and their mother going to the 1938 World's Fair

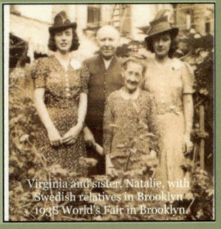
Virginia and sister, Natalie, with Swedish relatives in Brooklyn. 1938 World's Fair in Brooklyn.

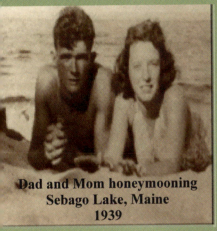
Dad and Mom honeymooning Sebago Lake, Maine 1939

On the beach Mom and Dad

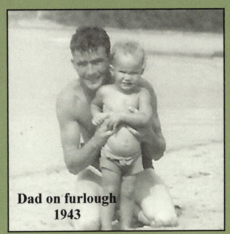
Dad on furlough 1943

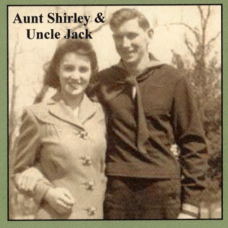
Aunt Shirley & Uncle Jack

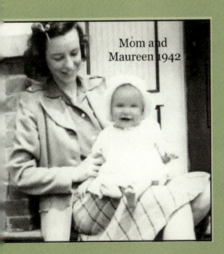
Mom and Maureen 1942

1944

A dress brought home from Italy

Dad carried this photo in his wallet throughout the war

The 50's and 60's

Maureen 1952
St. Pius School

Bonnie - 1952
St. Pius School

Michael age 6

Danny age 5

Bonnie
1960

Maureen
1961

Danny, Michael and Spot
Riverside RI, 1959

1980's

Bristol Rhode Island 2007
Cousins Mary, Emma, Madeleine, and Shea.
Virginia Hanson Bell's
memorial

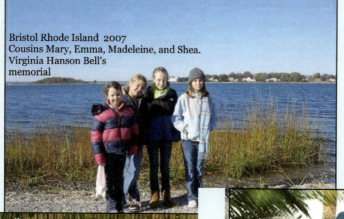

Ryan, Shane & Kerry
September 2001

The Head Family, 2017
Ryan & JD with John David & Virginia

Jensen Beach, Florida
Dawn and Drew's wedding
November 6, 1999

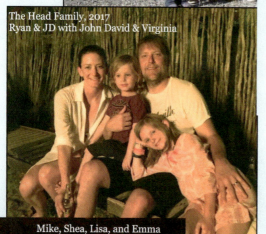

Mike, Shea, Lisa, and Emma

Madeleine, Kerry
& Mary
NYC 2015

San Juan Islands, Pacific Coast
Maureen, Drew, Dawn
Dave and Bonnie

Chapter VI: Aloha Dad

1938 Dad joined the Merchant Marines

The Parrot
Michael's Story

I gave Dad a blue hyacinth parrot for his birthday one year. It was given to me by a friend who imported them from Central America to Hawaii. Dad named the bird Paisano - "friend" in Italian. He had a special relationship with Paisano spending countless hours walking around the house and yard with his new friend perched on his hand or shoulder trying to teach him words.

Then one day Paisano took to the sky. Dad had overlooked the regular maintenance of clipping his flight feathers. Or maybe he thought it was cruel? Quite possible. Anyway, Dad would go out several times a day trying to coax him down from the roof or the fig tree or one of the many coconut trees surrounding our house. He tried really hard with food and "click-click" noises but Paisano would not come back down to Dad.

And then Paisano was gone. We never saw the bird again. But there is no reason to believe he did not make a home somewhere in Hawaii. After all, there are no natural predators, the climate is much like his natural habitat of the Amazon, and there would be plenty of food for him. In fact, even though parrots are not native to Hawaii, there are many escapees like Paisano seen in all parts of the island from the wild mountains to the banyan trees in the many public parks. Parrots are known to live to be 100 years - or older - which means that Paisano could still be flying around today in his early 70s!

Until he died I know that Dad would often check up in the coconut trees hoping that one day his parrot would come back. Far as we know, he never did. And I think that it must have made Dad somewhat sad. I know how he felt. I get a similar feeling when I visit Hawaii and walk down the beach to check out our old house. The deck on the beach where Mom and Dad sat just about every day is still there. We had great times - all of us - and I wish we could all be together to do that again.

But we cannot. Dad, Mom, Bonnie, and Dan have all taken flight too, and what's left are the many photos and sweet memories and stories that we will continue to pass down to our children and grandchildren.

As I write this story, a thought hits me . . . I wonder if Paisano ever has come back looking for Dad? Maybe he has.

I hope so . . . little jerk.

EULOGY - ROBERT EDWARD BELL
July 24, 1918 - April 24, 1989

On April 29, 1989, the family and friends of First Sgt. Robert E. Bell, United States Army, gathered together on a hilltop at the most beautiful and awe-inspiring National Memorial Cemetery of the Pacific. "Punchbowl" is the official resting place of more than 25,000 veterans who bravely fought for our country.

We stood silently at my father's gravesite as soldiers crossed the field in cadence. Suddenly they stopped, turned to the Pacific Ocean, raised their rifles, and from a distant hillside performed a 21 gun salute followed by Taps. To quote Michael, "It was eerily beautiful." Dad was then honored by the US State Department in recognition of his devoted and selfless contribution to the service of his country in WWII.

On that day at Punchbowl we knew for certain who our father was.

He was known as Dad, Grandpa, Bob, and Robbie. His men sometimes called him Sergeant Ding Dong. That's what happens when you're a Bell. His father Walter "Pop" was a good man — an Irish cop from Providence who loved his family, Narragansett beer, and The New York Yankees. On October 8th 1956 Pop took me to the World Series at Yankee Stadium. Don Larsen pitched a perfect game — one of baseball's most famous! Pop wrote songs and sang them on occasion - always on St. Paddy's Day. One song that I remember was about a girl from Riverside who stole my Dad's heart. Pop really liked my mother "Ginnie". Pop's wife Margaret Molloy "Maggie," died young. She was a devout Catholic, went to mass every morning and also enjoyed a day at the racetrack gambling with her friends. How I wish her grandchildren could have known her. Walter and Maggie had four sons — they all fought in WWII. Dad was the third to be born and the first to die.

Although he did not consider himself a war hero, we do know for certain that he came home from Italy with an impressive banner of stars and stripes and ribbons and medals - 4 bronze stars and an arrowhead. I believe the arrowhead had something to do with the battle at Anzio Bay where so many of his comrades were buried.

Dad was unique. He was creative and he was charming. He could tell a joke like no other. And he loved tricks. Our children would scream out and giggle as he would mysteriously make their favorite stuffed animal jump out of his arms, crawl across his belly, and sit on his shoulder. That's magic. I should not forget to add that he loved to cook Italian food. Yum. He left us a rich legacy of airplanes made out of beer cans and coconut heads which he carved with his pocket knife. They were strung up outside our door, which made us all laugh each time we sat outside on the beachfront lanai. Such good times. He was so proud of his family - an extraordinary gift to each and every one of us. Mom and Dad were together for a very long time. But not long enough. She was his heart and soul.

We are sure going to miss him. Aloha Dad.

So long Lake Garda. . .
   . . . See Ya Dad.

Dear Family,

It has been challenging to write the story of my father's war in Italy. You have been my inspiration. I know that he would not only want his family to be proud of him but also to be proud of all the soldiers - his brothers - who fought so bravely by his side. I have no doubt that the future generations of the Bell family will be reading and studying WWII and the battles of First Sgt. Robert E. Bell. You may even want to visit Italy one day and walk in his footsteps. I hope you do.

Special acknowledgments to Suzanne Becker and Colleen Kelly who took me to the finish line. I honestly could not have accomplished this major feat without their talents and perseverance.

Thank you to my granddaughter Virginia for her enthusiasm and contributions throughout this journey.

About The Author

St. Patrick's Day - New York City

Maureen Bell Broglia lives in Ridgewood, NJ, the mother of three daughters, and the grandmother of three girls and one boy.

She was born in Providence, RI, on the eve of the historic *Day of Infamy* -the bombing of Pearl Harbor. Her father fought in WWII in the Italian Campaign. He loved Italy and the warmth and hospitality of the people who welcomed the American soldiers into their country. His infantry - The Fifth - marched through the entire country "the boot" from Salerno, Anzio, Naples and Rome to Florence and Milan crossing the Apennines to eventual victory in May of 1945.

The V-Mails, photographs and memorabilia which he brought home from North Africa and Italy have deeply impacted her life.

CPSIA information can be obtained at www.ICGtesting.com
Printed in the USA
BVIW12n1804290818
525788BV00002B/2